Your Body for Life

Exercise

From birth to old age

Andrew Solway

Heinemann
LIBRARY
Chicago, Illinois

© 2013 Heinemann Library

an imprint of Capstone Global Library, LLC

Chicago, Illinois

Visit our web site at www.heinemannraintree.com

Edited by Andrew Farrow, Adam Miller, and Adrian Vigliano

Designed by Cynthia Della-Rovere

Original illustrations © Capstone Global Library Ltd.

Illustrated by HL Studios Ltd.

Picture research by Mica Brancic

Production by Victoria Fitzgerald

Originated by Capstone Global Library Ltd.

Printed and bound in China by Leo Paper Products Ltd.

16 15 14 13 12

10 9 8 7 6 5 4 3 2 1

Library of Congress Cataloging-in-Publication Data

Solway, Andrew.

  Exercise : from birth to old age / Andrew Solway.

    p. cm.—(Your body for life)

  Includes bibliographical references and index.

  ISBN 978-1-4329-7083-3 (hb)—ISBN 978-1-4329-7090-1 (pb)
1. Exercise. 2. Physical fitness. 3. Health. I. Title.

RA781.S6238 2013

613.7—dc23   2012014477

Acknowledgments

The author and publishers are grateful to the following for permission to reproduce copyright material: Alamy pp. 6 (© epa european pressphoto agency b.v), 12 (© Bernhard Classen), 21 (© Bob Daemmrich), 28 (© Bubbles Photolibrary), 29 (© Enigma), 30 (© Terry Foster), 51 (© Juice Images), 53 (© diyiming), 54 (© piluhin), 19 top left (© Janine Wiedel Photolibrary/Jacky Chapman); Corbis pp. 24 (© Image Source), 42 (© Robert Michael), 47 (TempSport/© Jean-Yves Ruszniewski); Getty Images p. 26 (Taxi/Justin Pumfrey); iStockphoto p. 35 (© Jonathan Downey); Science Photo Library p. 50 (Dept. Of Anatomy/Prof. P. Motta); Shutterstock pp. 4 (© Jaochainoi), 5 (© Dmitry Kalinovsky), 11 (© Val Thoermer), 16 (© manzrussali), 20 (© muzsy), 22 (© swinner), 22 (© Andrei Nekrassov), 22 (© pryzmat), 22 (© BMCL), 22 (© Volodymyr Krasyuk), 23 (© Carlos E. Santa Maria), 25 (© Jiang Dao Hua), 31 (© testing), 32 (© auremar), 36 (© Audrey Snider-Bell), 37 (© Gertjan Hooijer), 38 (© Aspen Photo), 40 (© Geir Olav Lyngfjell), 43 (© Flashon Studio), 46 (© Monkey Business Images), 14 bottom left (© Jaroslaw Grudzinski), 14 top right (© Kenishirotie), 19 bottom right (© maska);

Cover photograph of dumbells reproduced with permission of Shutterstock (© Peter vd Rol).

Cover photograph of a young woman running near the sea reproduced with permission of Shutterstock (© Dmitriy Shironosov).

We would like to thank David Wright for his invaluable help in the preparation of this book.

Every effort has been made to contact copyright holders of any material reproduced in this book. Any omissions will be rectified in subsequent printings if notice is given to the publisher.

Disclaimer

All the Internet addresses (URLs) given in this book were valid at the time of going to press. However, due to the dynamic nature of the Internet, some addresses may have changed, or sites may have changed or ceased to exist since publication. While the author and publisher regret any inconvenience this may cause readers, no responsibility for any such changes can be accepted by either the author or the publisher.

Contents

Some words are printed in **bold**, like this. You can find out what they mean by looking in the glossary on page 60.

Keeping Strong and Healthy

Do you get much exercise? Perhaps you play sports or are active in gym class at school. Maybe you do not play formal sports, but you kick a ball around at the park or in your backyard. Perhaps you enjoy dancing or running around with your dog. Maybe you spend a lot of time on your bike. There are lots of different ways to get exercise.

No need for exercise!

In less economically developed countries, the majority of people work on the land, growing food and raising animals. Producing enough food to feed a family, and having somewhere for them to live, involves long hours of hard physical work. People in these places get plenty of "exercise." But to be healthy, they also need things like a varied diet, safe drinking water, and medical care.

In the more economically developed world, most people do not have to do hard physical work to get food, warmth, and shelter. At work or in school, many people spend the majority of their time either standing or sitting down. For most journeys of any distance, they travel by car, bus, train, or plane, which means more sitting down. Because of the way we live, most of us do not do enough physical activity to keep our bodies healthy and strong. This is where exercise comes in.

Subsistence farmers

Subsistence farmers are people who can grow only enough food to feed themselves and their families. Such people cannot afford farm machinery, so growing and harvesting their crops is hard physical labor. These subsistence farmers in Thailand are harvesting rice.

The benefits of exercise

Exercise is essential to make our bodies work properly. If we do not exercise, our muscles become weak, our bones get thin and fragile, and we are likely to gain weight and even become **obese**. People who are obese are more at risk of suffering from all kinds of illnesses, from heart disease to **diabetes**.

Exercise makes your body do work. It uses your muscles, which need energy to function. It also gets your heart beating more quickly, which makes blood flow faster throughout the body. You also breathe faster and more deeply during exercise.

Changing bodies

In this book, you will learn more about the changes in the body from birth through old age. Exercise is good for us throughout life, even when we are babies or very old. But as the body changes, the kinds of exercise that work best for us change, too. When can we best improve our balance and **coordination**? When can we benefit most from **strength training**? When do we start to lose muscle? Can we do anything about it?

You can find the answers to all these questions and many more as you read through this book.

Big machines

In more developed countries, farm machinery has made growing food much less work. A farmer cutting wheat by hand can only harvest about two acres a day. A combine like this can harvest the same area in 12 minutes.

How the body moves

It seems simple, doesn't it? You decide you want to walk, run, or ride your bike. Your brain tells your muscles what to do, some muscles **contract**, others relax, and off you go.

Actually, it is a lot trickier than that. Even the simplest exercise involves most of the body's **organ systems**. For a start, your **skeletal system** is essential if you want to move. Bones provide anchor points for your muscles, and **joints** give you a wide range of movement.

You also need your **nervous system** to send instructions to the muscles and get feedback from them. Getting your muscles to do what you want is very tricky. You might think that you are consciously controlling what happens, but you are not really controlling it. A part of the brain called the cerebellum does a lot of the work without you knowing anything about it.

Muscle power
Chinese weight lifter Xiaojun Lu lifted 452 pounds (205 kilograms) during the 2011 World Championships. Weight lifters train to build muscles that give explosive power.

Energy for moving

So far we have gotten three organ systems involved. But that is just the start of the story. When your muscles contract, they do work, which means you are using energy. The energy has to come from somewhere. Like most other animals, humans get their energy from food. This involves a whole set of other organ systems.

First, the **digestive system** breaks down the food we eat into two basic groups. Useful **nutrients** are absorbed into the body, and waste materials are released in feces (solid waste).

Next, the **circulatory system** transports nutrients to the places in the body where they are needed. The nutrient that the muscles need is the sugar **glucose**. This is the main energy supply for the **cells**.

The muscles need one other ingredient to get energy from glucose, and that is oxygen. Without oxygen, the body can only get a fraction of the energy locked up in the tiny bits of glucose called molecules. The **respiratory system** draws air into the lungs, where oxygen can be absorbed quickly into the blood. The circulatory system then transports the oxygen to the muscles. (See page 9 for artwork showing these organ systems.)

Levers

Muscles, bones, and joints work together like **levers**. A lever is a rigid rod—in this case, a bone—that moves on a pivot (a joint). On one end of the lever is a load that needs to be moved. The muscle provides the force (called the effort) needed to move the load.

Some levers are used to give a mechanical advantage. This means that a small effort at one end of the lever can move a larger load at the other end. The muscles that contract when you stand on your toes work this way.

Other levers give a movement advantage. In this case, the effort is greater than the load, but a small movement of the effort (the muscle) moves the load a greater distance. The biceps muscle in the arm works this way. A small muscle movement moves the hand (the other end of the lever) a long distance.

Levers for lifting

The diagram shows one type of weight lifting lift, the snatch. The arms, legs, and hips act as pivots, with the bones working as levers. The muscles supply the force to make the levers move.

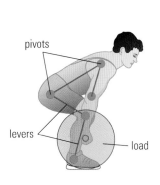

pivots

levers

load

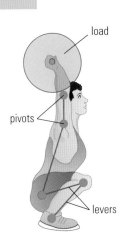

load

pivots

levers

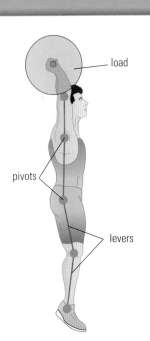

load

pivots

levers

Cells, tissues, organs, and organ systems

The human body is pretty well organized.

Cells are the smallest building blocks of the body. They are microscopic little capsules of chemicals. Different kinds of cells are specialized to do different jobs. Nerve cells, for example, carry tiny electric signals, while muscle cells are designed to contract.

Tissues are made up of large numbers of cells of a similar type. Muscle tissue, for example, is made up mainly of muscle cells. Epithelium is a tissue that covers and protects other tissue. It is made up of flattened epithelial cells.

Organs are body parts designed to do a particular job. The heart, for example, pushes blood around the body, while the stomach stores and breaks down food that has just entered the body. Organs are usually made up of several different types of tissue. The tissues all work together to enable the organ to do its job in the body.

Organ systems are groups of organs with similar functions working together. The heart is part of the circulatory system, which is concerned with supplying blood to all parts of the body. The stomach is part of the digestive system, which breaks down food.

Systems and functions

Muscular system

Main organs: Muscles, **tendons**

Muscles are tissues that can contract and relax.

Energy is needed for muscles to contract.

Contractions produce movement.

Skeletal system

Main organs: Bones, joints

Other tissues include cartilage and **ligaments**.

The skeleton is a framework that supports the body.

Joints allow parts of the body to move.

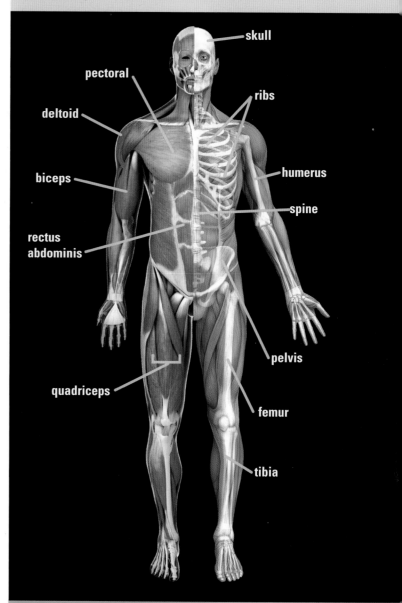

skull

pectoral

ribs

deltoid

biceps

humerus

spine

rectus abdominis

pelvis

quadriceps

femur

tibia

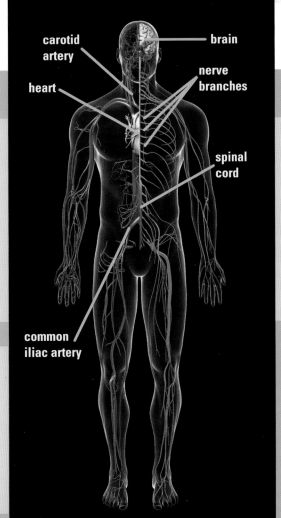

Circulatory system

Main organs: Heart, blood vessels (arteries, veins, capillaries)

The circulatory system carries food and oxygen to the body cells and carries away waste material.

carotid artery

heart

brain

nerve branches

spinal cord

common iliac artery

Nervous system

Main organs: Brain, **spinal cord**, peripheral nerves

The nervous system transmits impulses ("messages") rapidly throughout the body. This allows the body to respond to **stimuli** from inside and outside.

Organ systems

The diagrams show some of the body's main exercise-related organ systems—the muscular and skeletal systems, the circulatory and nervous systems, the respiratory system, and the digestive system.

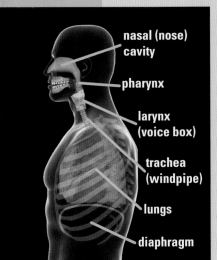

nasal (nose) cavity

pharynx

larynx (voice box)

trachea (windpipe)

lungs

diaphragm

Respiratory system

Main organs: Nose and mouth, trachea, bronchi and bronchioles (airways within the lungs), alveoli (microscopic air pockets at ends of bronchioles)

The respiratory system allows oxygen to enter the blood and **carbon dioxide** (waste) to pass out.

Digestive system

Main organs: Mouth, stomach, small intestine, large intestine

Other organs: Teeth, tongue, liver, pancreas

The digestive system breaks down food into a few simple types of nutrients that the body can use.

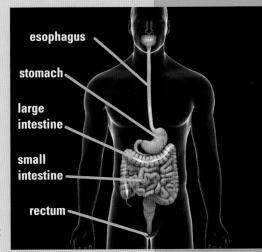

esophagus

stomach

large intestine

small intestine

rectum

Changes during exercise

We have looked at the different organ systems that are involved in exercise. But what happens when you actually start to exercise? How do the different systems react? Let's look at an example to find out.

Do you ride your bike to school? Let's suppose that most days you ride in with a couple of friends. But one morning, you are late. You get to the normal meeting place, but your friends have already left. You will have to really step on it to get to school on time!

You jump on your bike and start to pedal hard. Your heart starts to beat faster and more strongly. You can feel your heart really thumping in your chest.

You also start to breathe faster and more deeply. Soon you are gasping for breath. You cannot keep this speed up much longer. You are also feeling very hot and sweaty. Luckily, you are nearly there. You swing around the final corner and in through the school gates. You made it—just in time! Look at the photo on the right to see all of the work the body does when you ride a bicycle.

Turning on the power

The description above gives an idea of how much has to happen in the body to allow you to pedal faster. All these changes are geared towards producing enough energy in the place where it is needed—the muscles.

The muscles, and all the other cells in the body, get energy from food through a process called respiration. This is a series of chemical reactions that happen inside the cells. During normal respiration (**aerobic respiration**), glucose is broken down into carbon dioxide and water, and energy is released. The whole process is similar to combustion (burning), but broken down into lots of small, controllable steps.

When you exercise, your muscles contract faster and more strongly. This needs more energy, so respiration happens faster. More glucose is broken down, oxygen is used more quickly, and more carbon dioxide is produced. Your heart rate rises and you breathe faster in order to speed up the processes of getting oxygen and glucose to the muscles, and getting rid of waste carbon dioxide.

Respiration

Respiration is probably the most important set of chemical reactions in the world. Without it there would be no life. Respiration happens in all living things, from the tiniest bacteria to the biggest whales.

5. Your heart starts beating faster and more strongly. This pumps more blood around the body.

1. Your leg muscles start working hard, pushing the bike pedals around. This takes more energy than your muscles normally use.

2. The muscle cells need more glucose for energy. They also need more oxygen to get energy from the glucose. They take up extra glucose and oxygen from the blood.

3. The muscles also have to get rid of carbon dioxide, which is a waste product of energy production. The carbon dioxide is transported away in the blood.

4. The amounts of glucose and oxygen in the blood start to fall, while the amount of carbon dioxide goes up.

6. Blood flows more quickly through the blood vessels in your lungs. As you take faster, deeper breaths, more oxygen passes from the lungs into the blood. More carbon dioxide can also pass out of the blood and into the lungs.

7. As your muscles work, they produce heat as well as movement. You get hotter. **Glands** in the skin produce sweat to help cool you down.

8. There is only a limited supply of blood glucose. As this supply runs out, the liver gets involved in the action. The liver has a store of a carbohydrate called glycogen, made of long chains of glucose. When blood levels of glucose fall, the liver breaks down some of this glycogen into glucose.

Biking and the body

Most of your body's organ systems get involved as you ride on your bike.

Infancy:
From Wriggling to Walking

Before babies are born, they develop in a mother's womb. For the last couple of months before birth, the space is pretty tight—there is no room for exercise! So, when babies are born, they cannot do much. Newborn babies can wriggle and cry, open and close their hands, grasp a finger, and suck milk. But they cannot ride a bike, run or jump, or tie a knot. Babies' muscles and their muscle control are not well developed.

Water babies

Young babies who are placed in water will hold their breath and make swimming movements. They cannot actually swim, but in an emergency this swim reflex could make the difference between surviving and drowning.

For young babies, almost everything is a kind of exercise. Very young babies do not have neck muscles strong enough to hold up their head. So, even trying to look around is exercise. In the first year of life, babies learn to roll, crawl, hold things, reach out and pick things up, stand up, sit down, and maybe even walk. That is quite an exercise program!

Although young babies seem helpless, they have a whole range of **reflexes** to help them survive. One of the most obvious is the rooting reflex. If a baby is hungry and you touch its cheek, it will automatically turn its head toward you and try to suck your finger. This reflex helps babies feed from their mothers.

Another example is the startle reflex. If a baby's head is moved suddenly, it will throw its arms and legs wide, then pull the arms in again, and start to cry. This reflex probably helped with survival when parents carried their babies all the time. If the baby slipped and began to fall, the reflex helped the baby to cling on, and the crying drew the parent's attention.

Inside to outside, big to small

The development of a baby's muscles happens in a particular order. In general, the large muscles develop before the smaller ones. So, babies can wave their arms around before they learn fine control of the fingers. And they learn to walk, which requires large muscles, before they learn to control the small muscles that we use to talk:

- Generally, muscles develop from the core of the torso outward. This makes sense, because the **core muscles** are the ones that maintain **posture**.

- At first, babies mostly use the muscles in their face, to communicate through facial expressions and sounds. Next, they start using the neck, shoulder, and arm muscles to look around, reach for things, and hold on. Later, they use the lower body and leg muscles more, as they learn to crawl and then walk.

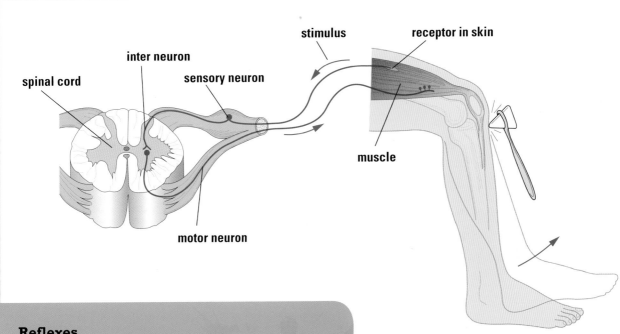

Reflexes

A reflex is when the body automatically responds to a stimulus. For example, if you accidentally touch something hot, your hand will jerk away from it without you having to think about it.

Reflexes literally happen without thought. In the heat example, a message from the heat receptors in your fingers travels up a nerve to your spinal cord. Normally, the message would go on to the brain. But in a reflex, the message triggers a set response. A message travels along another nerve to muscles in your arm. They contract and pull the arm away from the hot object. The whole process happens very quickly.

Reflex action

The knee-jerk reflex is often used by doctors to test a patient's reflexes. Tapping lightly on the knee ligament causes the quadriceps muscle in the upper leg to lengthen suddenly. This produces a reflex action in which the quadriceps contracts and the lower leg jerks upwards.

Wriggling and walking

Babies' "walking" reflex disappears at about six weeks old, but then, from about six months onward, babies start learning to walk for real.

Have you ever played with a doll or an action figure? If you have, you will probably have noticed that it is pretty hard to make it stand up. Balancing a tall figure on two small feet is quite a task. For humans, standing and walking are tough, too. Learning to walk is one of the biggest achievements of early life.

Learning to walk

The first stage of learning to walk is rolling. By six months, most babies can roll from their back onto their front, and from front to back again. Some babies get really good at this and roll themselves around the room!

The next stage in the process is getting onto the hands and knees. From there, babies soon learn to crawl. Now they can really begin to move around. Many babies spend quite a long time at this stage, crawling to get around and sitting when they want to use their hands or look around.

From rolling to cruising

The baby in the top photo can roll onto his front, lift himself up on his arms and look around. The baby in the lower photo has learned to stand and is "cruising" from place to place.

Long before they are ready to walk, babies start to exercise their legs. Babies lying on their back enjoy kicking their legs, and if you press on their feet, they will push back against your hands. By about six months old, most babies can stand on your lap when you support them, and they soon begin to bounce up and down in this position. All this is good exercise for the muscles they will need for walking.

Going from crawling to walking is the trickiest stage. A lot of children are 15 to 18 months old before they start to walk. The first stage is to move from crawling to standing. This involves using a lot of new muscles and improving balance. Often babies will hold on to something for support when they begin to stand.

From standing, the final stage is the development of walking. This involves coordination as well as balance. Often babies begin by "cruising"—moving around the room holding on to furniture. Finally, they learn to walk without holding on to anything.

Try this

Can you stand completely still? Try this activity and find out.

Use a headband or a scarf to fasten a felt-tip pen to the back of your head, with the point upward. Get a friend to hold a piece of cardboard above your head so that the point of the pen is just touching it. Now try to stand perfectly still for 30 seconds. Afterward, look at the cardboard. What do you see?

You will probably find that the pen has drawn wiggly lines on the cardboard, because you were not standing still. When we stand, our muscles are constantly adjusting to keep us balanced and upright, but we do not usually notice this.

Walking robots

If you want to know how difficult walking is, ask a robot! Most traveling robots move on wheels or tracks. It is relatively easy to build robots that move in this way. Bipedal (two-legged walking) robots are so complex that they can't really do anything other than walk.

Swimming

Swimming is one of the first activities babies can learn. There are parent and baby swimming classes for babies as young as six weeks.

Starting young
This young boy is learning to swim. Swimming is a good exercise for developing the heart and lungs, and for improving flexibility.

Babies can swim early because they do not need to be able to walk before they can get in the water. Swimming is a low-impact activity, which means that it does not cause wear and tear on weight-bearing joints such as the knees and hips.

For older children and adults, swimming has other benefits as a form of exercise. Water is harder to move through than air. To swim quickly, we have to work hard, which involves using muscles throughout the body. So, swimming is good for overall fitness. It also makes people more flexible, improves coordination, and gets the heart and lungs working hard. Because it is low-impact, swimming is a good exercise for older people as well as for babies.

The science of swimming

When we swim, the water offers more resistance to movement than air does. This resistance is called **drag**. Top swimmers and coaches have worked with scientists to find ways to reduce drag and swim faster. Scientific studies have led to changes in the way that swimmers do the different strokes.

Science has also helped with swimsuit design. Many top swimmers wear swimsuits made of a special material based on studies of sharks and their skin. Shark skin has a surface of tiny, rough scales. Surprisingly, water flows better over these scales than over a smooth surface. So, the swimsuit material has ridges in it that are designed to give a smoother water flow around the swimmer and thus reduce drag.

AMAZING BUT TRUE!

Ice cold

British swimmer Lewis Pugh has swum in some of the coldest water in the world in just swimming trunks, goggles, and a swimming cap. In 2005, he swam 0.62 mile (1 kilometer) in both the Arctic and the Antarctic oceans. He is the only person to have completed long-distance swims in all the world's oceans—the Arctic, the Atlantic, the Indian, the Pacific, and the Southern oceans.

AMAZING BUT TRUE!

Golden swimmer

The swimmer who has won the most world titles and Olympic medals is Michael Phelps of the United States. At the 2008 Olympics in Beijing, China, Phelps won eight gold medals. This is the most gold medals won by any athlete in one games. Phelps has won 14 Olympic golds in total, more than any other athlete.

A low-tech way that swimmers can improve their performance is to take a hot shower before a race. Taking a hot shower adds a little extra warmth, and many swimmers find that it improves their race performance.

This is different from a warm-up. It is important to warm up the muscles before exercising hard. Gentle exercise warms the muscles and increases the blood flowing to them, which helps to prevent injuries and stiffness after exercise. So, all athletes do some kind of active warm-up.

Childhood: Growing and Changing

After the first year or so, the speed at which babies grow slows down, but there is still plenty of growth and change during early childhood.

Running, jumping, and playing

Big head, short legs

As we develop, different parts of the body grow different amounts. A toddler has much shorter legs and a larger head compared to an adult. This means that a toddler's **center of gravity** is slightly higher than an adult's. Because of this, balancing while walking is slightly harder for a toddler than it is for an adult. However, toddlers' short legs and supple hip joints mean that if they do fall over, they are less likely to hurt themselves. They also don't have to fall as far!

If you watch a two-year-old walking, you can see why young children are often called toddlers. Walking is still a difficult activity for them. They seem to be almost falling from one foot to the other rather than walking smoothly. But by the age of four, children are much more confident physically. They can walk, run, jump, and perhaps ride a tricycle or a scooter.

The main way that children get exercise at this age is by playing. Running after a ball or a pet dog, skipping, playing on a jungle gym, climbing the steps of a slide, and going on the seesaw are all exercise. These activities improve strength, balance, and coordination.

Giving children a chance

Early childhood is the most important period for overall development. If a young child gets good nutrition (healthy food choices), care, and plenty of exercise, he or she has a good chance of growing up to be a healthy, intelligent adult.

More than 200 million children under five years old do not get the basic things they need for the healthy development of their bodies and brains. They suffer from a lack of food over long periods. They may lack specific nutrients such as iron (an important part of the blood). They also do not get enough exercise or education. This is a particular problem in South Asia and much of Africa.

Finer movements

As they get older, children continue to develop their physical skills. Older children can ride a bicycle, pump themselves upward on a swing, climb a climbing net, swing on monkey bars, and do many other things that a toddler cannot manage.

From about the age of four onward, children learn better fine control of their muscles. They can do things like color and draw, tie shoelaces, fasten and unfasten buttons, sew, or use a keyboard. Children also learn skills quickly at this age. This is a good time to start learning a musical instrument, for example.

Playground skills

By the age of four or five, children have the balance, strength, and coordination to get the most out of a visit to the playground.

Nimble fingers

Tying shoelaces involves much more accurate muscle control than using playground equipment. This fine control takes longer to develop.

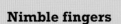

Team sports

Most children start school at around four years old. They spend less time with their parents and more time with other children. From about five or six years old onward, they can learn new physical skills through coaching and instruction from their parents and teachers as well as through playing or copying. This is when many children get involved in sports, especially team sports.

Part of the team
Playing team sports involves a whole range of physical and mental skills. Players have to be able to assess what is happening around them, plan ahead, work with teammates and avoid the opposition.

Ball skills
Team sports often involve ball skills— throwing and catching or hitting a ball. These kinds of skills need hand–eye coordination. Actually, a better name for this would be eye–body coordination. This is a complex process. Suppose you want to catch a ball coming toward you. Your brain has to process information coming from your senses, mainly your eyes, about the flight of the ball. It uses this information to send out signals to the muscles in your body. The muscles move the body into roughly the right position to catch the ball. As the ball gets closer, the brain continues sending out signals to the muscles. The arms and hands make small adjustments to be in the right place to catch the ball as it arrives. Your ears are important, too, because the organs that help you to balance are part of your ears.

Team sports are one of the most common ways that children in school get exercise. Most people take part in team activities at some time. These could be more casual kinds of team activities, such as playing tag or throwing a Frisbee in the park, or something more organized, such as being on a school team for soccer or hockey.

Young children cannot throw and catch well. People develop this ability as their bodies become better coordinated. Ball skills also take a lot of practice.

Training

As children get older, they might start to focus more on specific kinds of exercise that they enjoy. Some kids might like team games like basketball or soccer, while others like individual ball games such as tennis or golf. Some kids might be good at swimming or enjoy gymnastics. Others could be more interested in dancing, going on bike rides, or other activities that are not as sporty.

Many older children spend a lot of time training for their favorite sport or activity. There are two main kinds of training for most physical activities. The first is to improve general fitness. The second is skills training, which is specific to that particular sport or activity.

For many sports, circuit training is often used to improve general fitness. This involves doing a series of activities, spending about 30 seconds or 1 minute on each activity. Circuits can be designed to develop the best kind of fitness for a particular sport. A circuit designed for football, for example, might include exercises to build strength, for scrimmages and tackles, and speed, for running with the ball.

Wheelchair basketball

Wheelchair basketball is a fast-paced and exciting game. More than 100,000 people play the game and 82 countries have national teams.

Keeping safe

Toddlers spend a lot of their time with parents or other caregivers, who make sure that they are safe while they are playing. As children get older, they spend more time doing activities with other children or in groups with one or two adults looking after them. Older children also do activities that are more dangerous, such as BMX riding, skateboarding, and horse riding. Activities in which there is more risk of injury need safety equipment.

One very useful piece of safety equipment is a crash helmet. Without a helmet, a fall from a horse or from the top of a half-pipe could cause a serious injury. Other kinds of safety gear include knee and elbow pads, to protect the joints, and goggles or helmet visors, to protect the eyes. Different kinds of sports need different safety equipment.

Safety equipment

Some common pieces of safety equipment include:

- *Helmet*: For biking, skateboarding, baseball and softball, inline skating, skiing, and snowboarding
- *Goggles or visor*: For ice hockey, snowboarding, football, baseball and softball (when batting)
- *Mouth guard*: For martial arts, boxing, wrestling, and football
- *Knee and elbow pads*: For skateboarding, BMX, mountain biking, and rollerblading
- *Other pads*: For football, hockey, ice hockey, and baseball
- *Shoes*: Special shoes are important for safety in most sports and physical activities, including soccer, football, track and field, climbing, and horse riding.

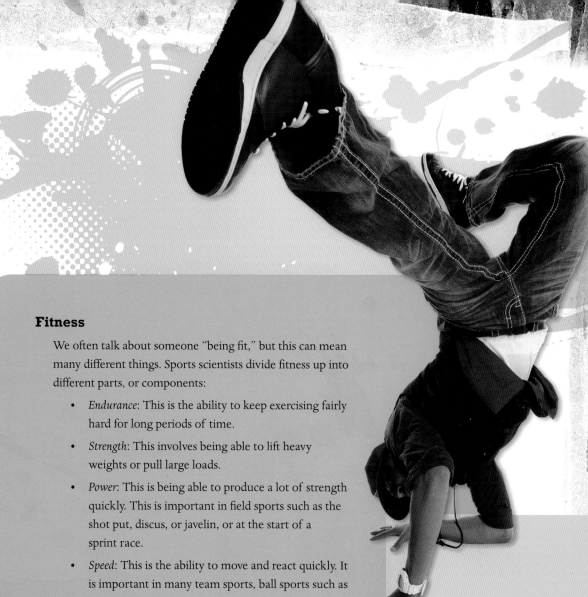

Fitness

We often talk about someone "being fit," but this can mean many different things. Sports scientists divide fitness up into different parts, or components:

- *Endurance*: This is the ability to keep exercising fairly hard for long periods of time.

- *Strength*: This involves being able to lift heavy weights or pull large loads.

- *Power*: This is being able to produce a lot of strength quickly. This is important in field sports such as the shot put, discus, or javelin, or at the start of a sprint race.

- *Speed*: This is the ability to move and react quickly. It is important in many team sports, ball sports such as tennis and squash, and in martial arts.

- *Agility*: This means being able to accelerate (start and stop) and change direction quickly and accurately. This is an important part of many sports.

- *Flexibility*: This involves the range of movement people have in their joints. It is an important type of fitness for dance, gymnastics, swimming, and similar kinds of exercise. Flexibility training also helps to protect against injury in all kinds of exercise.

- *Coordination*: This is the ability to combine the action of various parts of the body in a controlled manner. It is an important part of all ball sports, gymnastics, dance, and many other activities.

- *Balance*: This is the ability to control the body position without falling over. It is particularly important in sports such as gymnastics.

Fit for action

Sports are not the only way to exercise and get fit. Dance moves like this require strength, agility, flexibility, balance, and coordination.

Gymnastics

Most people who become really good at gymnastics, dance, or cheerleading start early. All three activities need high levels of balance, agility, and flexibility. These are skills that people develop quite early in life. For example, we reach our maximum level of flexibility at about eight years old.

Exercises to improve flexibility are of most benefit at this age. However, it is important not to overdo this stretching, because the bones and muscles are still growing and gaining strength. Over-stretching the muscles or trying to do too much strength training can cause long-term damage. For all these kinds of exercise, good coaching and guidance are extremely important.

Top gymnasts develop incredible skills of balance and agility. One gymnastic event for female gymnasts is the beam. Gymnasts on the beam must perform their whole routine, which often involves jumps and somersaults, on a beam that is just 4 inches (10 centimeters) wide. To avoid losing their balance, their center of gravity must remain over the beam throughout the routine.

AMAZING BUT TRUE!

Nadia Comaneci

One of the greatest female gymnasts of all time was Nadia Comaneci. Her gymnastic talents were spotted when she was just six years old, and she began regular training with coach Bela Karolyi. She came in 13th place at the Romanian National Junior Gymnastics Championships at the age of seven and won 1st place the next year, at age eight.

In 1976, at the age of 14, Nadia became the youngest gymnast ever to win the all-around Olympic gold medal. She also won gold on the beam and the uneven bars. During the competition, she became the first gymnast to get a perfect score of 10 in Olympic gymnastics. This was so unusual that the scoreboard could not cope. It showed her score as 1.00 instead of 10.00. She was fortunate to not suffer major health problems despite all her training. She now runs a gymnastics school with her husband in Oklahoma.

Power and strength

Many gymnastic exercises require strength as well as agility. Strength is especially emphasized in male gymnastics. For example, male gymnasts often do moves such as pushing up from bent arms into a handstand or holding themselves out on the rings with arms straight out, in a "cross" position. People reach their maximum strength in young adulthood (see page 38), and many experts think it is not safe to do much strength training before this age. It is especially important not to overload the spine. So, top male gymnasts are often older than top females.

Over the top

The asymmetric bars are a tremendous challenge for young gymnasts. Flying off the top of the higher bar and catching the lower one requires agility, flexibility, strength—and a lot of courage!

Risks of gymnastics

In general, improving flexibility is good for the body. It improves performance and reduces the chance of injury in most kinds of exercise. However, it is possible to over-stretch joints, which can cause damage to muscles, tendons, and ligaments. It can also cause **arthritis** later in life. To avoid such problems, it is important not to overdo stretching exercises. Never "bounce" in a stretch, and do not push a stretch so far that it is painful.

Adolescence: A Period of Change

Around the age of 10, big changes start to happen in the body. This is when **puberty** begins. Puberty is the name for the changes that happen as we turn from children into adults, capable of reproducing (having babies). During puberty, the body changes more quickly than at any time after the first year of life. The period after the beginning of puberty is also called **adolescence**.

Timing of puberty

On average, girls start and complete puberty earlier than boys. For girls, the main changes happen between the ages of about 10 and 14, while for boys they begin a year or two later and continue until the age of 17 or 18.

Big differences

Although the average age for puberty to start is around the age of 10 for girls and 11 to 12 for boys, there are big differences in the timing among individuals. For girls, puberty can start as early as 8 or as late as 16. For boys, it can start from about 10 or it might not begin until 14.

Who grows first?

Because girls begin puberty earlier, they start their growth spurt earlier. In a group of young people between the ages of 12 and 13, the girls will generally be taller than the boys.

This table shows some of the main physical changes that may occur during puberty	
Males	**Females**
Grow taller	Grow taller
Muscles increase in mass and strength	Development of breasts
Bones and skull get heavier	Hips and pelvis become wider, to aid in childbirth
Growth of hair on face, under arms, on chest, and around penis	Growth of body hair under arms and around vagina
Penis and testes (male sex glands) increase in size and the production of sperm (reproductive cells) begins	Ovaries (female **reproductive organs**) begin producing eggs
Larynx gets larger and voice deepens	Menstrual cycles (periods) start
Chest becomes broader	Waist remains smaller than in men
Lower amounts of body fat than females	More subcutaneous fat (fat layer beneath the skin) than in males

Physical changes

The main changes that take place during puberty are in the reproductive organs, which grow bigger and become active. These changes are essential for our survival. If we could not reproduce, the whole human race would die out.

Many other changes happen at puberty. These changes are known as secondary sex characteristics. Both males and females begin to grow more hair on their bodies, and males also grow hair on their faces—they have to start shaving. Females grow breasts and their shape becomes more rounded. In males, the larynx (voice box) grows, making the voice deeper.

Even the way people smell changes. In both males and females, the skin produces more oils, and these change the smell of sweat. Oily skin can cause bouts of acne (pimples). However, these usually clear up as young people become adults.

Chemicals in the blood

The changes that happen during puberty are triggered by chemicals known as **hormones**. Small amounts of hormones are released into the blood. They travel through the bloodstream to target sites, where they have an effect. The uterus (womb) and the breasts are important target sites for female sex hormones.

Taller, broader, stronger

Some changes that happen during puberty affect how people exercise. During puberty, both boys and girls grow taller. This may happen gradually over the course of puberty. But it is more likely that **adolescents** (young people) will have one or more growth spurts, where they grow quickly over a short period of time. On average, boys grow more during puberty than girls. Because of this, men are generally taller than women.

Girls and boys grow differently during puberty. As girls grow into women, their hips get broader and their figure becomes more rounded. They also develop breasts, so that if they have a baby, they can feed it with nourishing milk. As boys become men, their shoulders grow broader, their bones become thicker, and their muscles get larger.

Moods and feelings

The hormones that produce physical changes also have an effect on the way that adolescents feel and behave during the period of puberty. There are big changes happening in the brain, too, and these can also affect behavior. Adolescents can have sudden mood swings, feeling on top of the world one minute and depressed the next. Young people worry about their appearance and what other people think of them. They are also often angry and aggressive. Many adolescents also experiment with potentially harmful activities such as smoking, drinking alcohol, or taking illegal drugs.

Smoking and drinking

Adolescence is a time when many people try out new things as they develop into adulthood. They may try alcohol for the first time and perhaps also smoke. This may cause health problems later in life (see page 42).

AMAZING BUT TRUE!

Moving puberty

The age at which puberty started was much later in the 19th century than it is today. In the 1840s, puberty in girls began between the ages of 15 and 17, compared to around the age of 10 for girls today. Research at the University of North Carolina suggests that the age of puberty for boys is also falling.

Scientists do not completely understand why these changes are happening. There are probably several reasons, such as increased **obesity** in young people and the presence of pollutants in the environment.

Training for strength

Puberty is a time when muscles grow and develop. The changes are bigger in males, but they happen in females, too. It is a time when young people can benefit from strength training. Before puberty, many experts advise against **resistance training** (weight training).

As with flexibility training, it is important not to overdo training for strength. Young people doing weight training should probably not try the kind of explosive lifting that weight lifters do. They should get expert help and work with proper equipment. Doing too much weight training, or lifting weights in the wrong way, can lead to back injuries, damage to muscles, and fractured bones. However, after the growth spurt in puberty, most adolescents can begin some resistance training to help increase strength without negative effects. This can also help to build strong bones, which can be of great benefit later in life.

Resistance is useful

Resistance bands are a simple, lightweight piece of equipment that can be used for strength training. The muscles have to work against the resistance created when the strong elastic in the resistance bands is stretched.

Case study: Sprint events

It is the 100-meter men's final in Berlin, Germany, in 2009. The starter says, "Set," and the sprinters rise up in their blocks like coiled springs. There is a breathless pause, then the starting gun cracks. The sprinters hurl themselves forward, heads down and legs pumping. By about 30 meters, the runners are upright and striding out. Suddenly, the tallest man in the field surges ahead, taking a lead of perhaps 2 meters. He keeps up his blistering pace to the end, finishing in a time of 9.58 seconds. Usain Bolt, the fastest sprinter in the world, has broken his own world record.

Usain Bolt was an exceptional sprinter from an early age. At age 12, he was the fastest sprinter at his school in Trelawney, Jamaica. In his early teens, two coaches encouraged him to focus on track and field rather than the sport cricket, and his race times improved enormously. In 2002, at age 15, he won the 200-meter World Junior Championships with a time of 20.61 seconds. At the 2008 Beijing Olympics, he won both the 100-meter and 200-meter sprints in world-record times. At the World Championships in Berlin in 2009 (mentioned above), he set world record times of 9.58 seconds for the 100 meters and 19.19 seconds for the 200 meters.

What is needed for speed

In a sprint, runners are looking to get the absolute maximum out of their muscles for a short period of time. In this situation, the muscles can use a special "booster" for extra power. This booster is called **anaerobic respiration**. Anaerobic means "without air," so anaerobic respiration can happen without the need for oxygen. With the help of anaerobic respiration, runners can get more power from their muscles over short periods.

Out of the blocks

A sprint start is a perfect example of explosive power.

Anaerobic drawbacks

Why don't our muscles use anaerobic respiration all the time? There are two reasons:

- First, anaerobic respiration is inefficient. It produces about one-18th the amount of energy produced by aerobic respiration (which needs oxygen).
- Second, the waste products affect muscle contraction. When people use the anaerobic booster, a waste product called lactic acid begins to build up. This quickly makes the environment inside the muscle cells more acidic. In acid conditions, the muscles cannot contract as fast or as strongly as normal, and muscle fatigue sets in. This means that the muscle tissue can no longer contract, because it has run out of glucose "fuel."

Fast and furious
People doing martial arts such as tae kwon do need the same kind of speed and explosive power as sprinters.

The muscles used for all kinds of exercise are called skeletal muscles, because they attach to the skeleton. We actually have two types—fast-twitch and slow-twitch. For sprinting, runners need lots of fast-twitch muscles, because they contract more quickly and produce more power.

The relative amounts of fast-twitch and slow-twitch muscle people have is **genetic**, meaning they are passed down in **genes** from parents. Some people are born with mainly fast-twitch muscles, some have mainly slow-twitch muscles, and most people are somewhere in between. Although people can develop and strengthen the fast-twitch muscles they have, it is not possible to develop more. So, people with a lot of fast-twitch muscles have a definite advantage when it comes to sprinting.

Couch potatoes versus gym bunnies

When adolescents get to the end of puberty, they are fully grown. This is more or less the end of physical development (although some people might gain some more muscle in the next few years). Some people think that now they are fully grown, they can stop getting exercise. Is this a good idea?

It is certainly true that once they leave school, many people pretty much stop exercising. But how bad is that really? Parents, teachers, and governments all insist that exercising is good, and that we shouldn't be couch potatoes. But what is wrong with a couch potato? Sitting around, relaxing, watching TV, and playing on the computer does not sound too awful. Maybe being a couch potato could be fun. And maybe exercise is not as good as it is cracked up to be.

Life balance
There's nothing wrong with relaxing and watching your favorite TV show from time to time. But when things get out of balance and people start spending too much time in front of a screen—and not enough time exercising—health hazards can start to develop.

Get off the couch!

So is it better to exercise, or to be a couch potato? Let's look at some evidence.

If young people spend hours sitting on the couch watching TV, or sitting in front of a computer or video game console, they are using less energy than if they are active. The muscles are not working much, so they become smaller and less powerful. It is also tempting to eat too much food while being a couch potato. Then young people end up gaining weight.

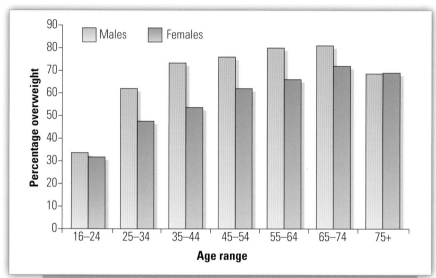

Weight problems at different ages

The graph shows the results of a survey conducted in England in 2006 to find out what percentage of males and females were overweight at different ages. Overall, about 20 percent of men and 14 percent of women have health problems due to being overweight.

Many studies by doctors and medical experts have found that overweight people have health problems. They are at greater risk of illnesses such as heart disease, hypertension (high blood pressure), high **cholesterol** levels, and type 2 diabetes (an illness caused by buildup of glucose in the blood). Being overweight can even lead to early death. At least 2.8 million people die each year because they are overweight or obese.

Just the facts

According to the World Health Organization:

- The number of people who are overweight or obese has more than doubled since 1980.
- In 2008, nearly 1.2 billion people worldwide were overweight.
- More than 1 in 10 adults is obese.

According to the U.S. Department of Health:

- More than 60 percent of U.S. adults do not get regular exercise.
- About 25 percent of U.S. adults are not active at all.

Assessing the evidence

In recent years, studies have shown that it is not just adults that are overweight. More and more young people are becoming overweight, too, as we will see on the next pages. Maybe being a couch potato is not such a good idea after all.

Obesity in young people

Teenagers spend a lot of time listening to music, hanging out with friends, surfing the Internet, playing computer games, and going to see movies or bands. In general, they spend a lot less time exercising than when they were younger. Teenagers are also more independent, so they often get their own meals or eat out more. Studies show that teens tend to eat more starchy and fatty foods, such as chips and hamburgers, perhaps because this kind of "fast food" is enjoyable to eat and easy to obtain. This combination of less exercise and an unbalanced diet can lead to young people becoming overweight.

Keeping it in the family

Studies have shown that people in the same family tend to have a similar diet and similar levels of physical activity. The best approach is for the whole family to work together to maintain a good diet and get plenty of exercise.

In many countries, more young people are overweight or obese than in the past. In the United States, around 1 in 3 children is obese—three times as many as in the 1960s. As we have already seen, being very overweight can cause health problems—for instance, painful joints, headaches, vision problems, high blood pressure, and high levels of blood fats. Many obese children also suffer from type 2 diabetes.

BMI

BMI stands for "body mass index." It is a measure of whether or not someone is a good weight for his or her height. The actual calculation is weight (in pounds) divided by height (in inches) squared, and then that number is multiplied by 703. You can figure out your BMI if you know your weight and height, or you can use a chart like the one shown here.

Although the BMI gives some indication of whether or not someone is overweight, it is not always very accurate. Muscles and bones are heavy, and both types of tissue are developed by exercise. So a muscular person with strong bones could have quite a high BMI.

A better measure is to work out the percentage body fat. Skin-fold tests are one way to measure this. The most accurate way is to weigh the body while submerged in water, but this method is slow and quite expensive.

The best way to avoid obesity is to eat a balanced diet and get plenty of exercise. Many governments now run campaigns to persuade people to eat better and exercise more. In the United States, for example, the government recommends that children should get at least 60 minutes of exercise each day.

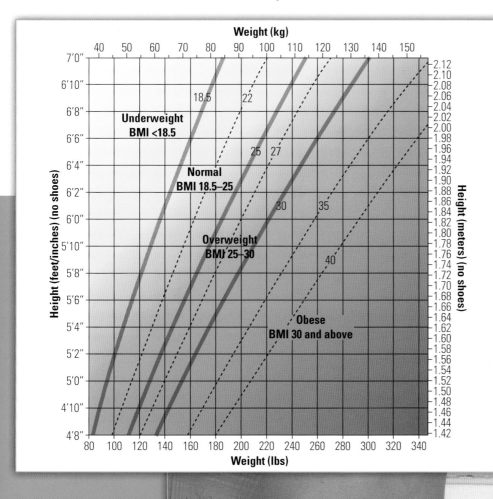

Weight (kg)

Height (feet/inches) (no shoes) / Height (meters) (no shoes)

Underweight BMI <18.5
Normal BMI 18.5–25
Overweight BMI 25–30
Obese BMI 30 and above

Weight (lbs)

BMI chart

This chart can be used to figure out BMI from your height and your weight. It is a rough guide as to whether or not someone is overweight.

Skin-fold testing

The photo shows a measurement being taken for a skin-fold test. This involves using a special tool that shows how much the skin can be folded at several sites on the body. Skin-fold tests can be used to give a rough estimate of how much excess fat a person's body is carrying.

Case study: Exercise is good for you!

People often say that if something is good for you, it cannot be any fun. But just about everyone has fun getting some kind of exercise. It could be a fun game on the playground, swimming in the ocean, jumping your bike over a ditch, dancing around to music, kicking a ball around, taking a picnic to the top of a hill, or just racing a friend to the end of the road.

And there is no doubt that exercise is good for you. It has so many benefits, it is like a miracle cure. Here are some examples of ways that exercise is good for you:

- *Exercise keeps your weight down*: We have seen that being overweight has health risks. If you exercise, you use more energy, and this helps to keep your weight down.

- *It boosts your energy*: If you exercise regularly, you have more energy for everyday activities. Over a whole day, you can only exercise at about one-fifth of your maximum. Any more than this and you will become exhausted. If you get plenty of exercise and are fairly fit, then a brisk walk will use only about a quarter of your maximum capacity. You could keep going for hours without getting really tired. But if you are unfit, going for a walk means exercising at half your maximum capacity. After only a short time, you will become tired and need to rest.

- *It combats illness*: Many studies have shown that exercise helps to prevent all kinds of illnesses.

- *It strengthens your heart*: This means you have less risk of getting heart disease.

- *It helps prevent viral illnesses*: This helps spare you from things such as colds, the flu, and chickenpox.

"Green" exercise

Any exercise is good, but recent studies seem to show that exercising in natural surroundings improves people's mood. The effects happen very fast: within the first five minutes, people start to feel good.

- *It helps to keep your arteries clear.* Arteries are tubes that help blood pass throughout the body. If the arteries are clear, this means you will not get an illness such as a **stroke** when you are older.

- *You have a much lower risk of bone and joint problems:* This prevents conditions such as arthritis.

- *You are less likely to get some types of cancer.* This is a major health problem to avoid.

- *It helps you to sleep:* Studies have shown that people who exercise regularly often sleep better and also get more refreshing sleep.

- *It stops you from dying early.* People who get regular exercise are 30 percent less likely to die early.

- *It cheers you up!:* Research has shown that physically active people recover from mild depression more quickly than people who do not exercise much. Exercise also stimulates the brain to release chemicals such as serotonin and endorphins, which can make you feel really great!

Hard work

This kind of exercise looks like hard work! However, the work is outside, and it strengthens the muscles, so it is likely to be good for your health.

This table shows the energy needed for different activities	
Main daily activities	**Relative energy cost**
Sleeping, resting	1
Sitting, reading, desk work	1–2
Sitting typing, playing piano, operating controls	1.5–3
Light work, gardening, slow walking	2–4
Social sports, cycling, tennis, baseball, light factory or farm work	3–6
Heavy physical labor, carrying, stacking, cutting wood, jogging, competitive sports	4–8.5
Very hard physical labor, intense physical activity, heavy lifting, very vigorous sports	over 10

Young Adulthood:
Peak Performance

Puberty usually ends at around the age of 17 for females and 18 for males. From this age until about 30, people are at the peak of their physical development. Young adults reach their maximum height in their early twenties and their peak strength in their late twenties. During this period in life, vision and hearing, manual agility (the ability to do things with the hands), and coordination are all excellent. Young adults are also less likely to get sick than at other times in life.

Expanding horizons

Because this is the time of peak physical development, nearly all top athletes are young adults. These elite athletes spend hours every day training for their sport or activity and reach levels of fitness and skill far beyond those of most people.

High achievers
By the time they are young adults, top athletes have done thousands of hours of training for their sport. They have tremendous physical skills and very high levels of fitness.

A training day

This is one day in the training schedule of top athlete Jessica Ennis. She competes in the heptathlon, which is a women's event in which athletes compete over two days in seven events—long jump, high jump, javelin, shot put, 100-meter hurdles, a 200-meter race, and an 800-meter race.

9 a.m	Track work—a hurdle session followed by high jump
12:30 p.m.	Lunch
2:30 p.m.	Afternoon training—shot put work followed by weights, then plyometrics, which involves short, fast exercises to sharpen reaction times
6 p.m.	Massage and soft-tissue treatment to ease aches
8 p.m.	Take the dog for a walk!

But people do not have to be elite athletes to enjoy exercise. Mountain biking, swimming, aerobics, hiking, and surfing are all popular with young adults, as well as ball sports such as soccer and tennis.

There are some basic principles for exercise training that anyone can use, whether they are a top athlete or just want to get in better shape:

- *Overload*: To get stronger muscles, you have to overload them. This means working your muscles harder than they are used to. Overloading muscles slightly damages the muscle fibers. This is part of why we feel stiff the day after hard exercise. But as the muscles repair themselves, they grow thicker and stronger.

- *Progression*: As your muscles get stronger, you have to exercise harder in order to keep overloading them. This is known as progression. A training program has to include progression, or athletes will get stuck at a certain fitness level.

- *Individuality*: Everyone's body reacts differently to exercise. An activity that quickly builds fitness in one person may have little effect in another.

- *Specificity*: Training has to be tailored to fit a particular sport or activity or body system. For example, training for gymnastics should include work on flexibility, balance, agility, and strength.

- *Recovery*: Recovery is essential to allow the body to rest. It is important that muscles have time to recover after each training session. This is why even top athletes do not train hard every single day. If you over-train, you will feel tired all the time and could cause permanent damage to your body.

With any strenuous activity, there is a risk of injury. Anyone who is concerned about an injury should stop exercise and seek professional medical advice.

Case study: Endurance

Most of us spend time on a bike at some point in our lives. But road cyclists spend hours riding at speeds beyond our fastest sprint. The most famous bike race is the Tour de France. It is one of the toughest of all sports events. Riders have to ride 20 stages in 22 days. Many of the stages are about 125 miles (200 kilometers) long, and nine of them are grueling rides in the mountains.

Tour de France riders need explosive energy and speed for the sprints that happen at various times during the race. However, more than anything, they need endurance—the ability to perform well for long periods of time. Endurance is also the top priority for people such as distance runners, mountaineers, hill walkers, and cross-country skiers.

Endurance athletes need to work aerobically. This means they have to get their energy from normal aerobic respiration, which needs oxygen. To get better at endurance sports, people have to improve the systems that deliver oxygen to the muscles—the respiratory system and circulatory system. Top endurance athletes have a slow heartbeat. Their heart is bigger and stronger than normal, so it can push more blood around the body in a single beat. They also have a bigger lung capacity—they can draw in more air in a single breath.

Hitting the trail

Mountain biking is just one of many endurance exercises that anyone can learn and enjoy. Hit the trail and have an adventure!

Maximum oxygen

A good measure of people's endurance fitness is how much oxygen they can take in within a set time (usually a minute). This measurement is known as maximal oxygen uptake, or $VO_{2\,max}$. An average young adult male has a $VO_{2\,max}$ of about 45. Elite male athletes can have a $VO_{2\,max}$ of over 80. Cross-country skier Bjørn Dæhlie has a $VO_{2\,max}$ of 96—and this was measured when he was not in training!

When reading about sprinting (see page 31), we learned about slow-twitch and fast-twitch muscles. Fast-twitch muscles are good for speed and power, but endurance athletes need lots of slow-twitch muscles. This type of muscle contracts less powerfully, but it can continue working for much longer.

AMAZING BUT TRUE!

Exercise makes a difference

Keeping fit and active makes a huge difference in your $VO_{2\,max}$. A fit and active 65-year-old can have a better $VO_{2\,max}$ than a 25-year-old who gets little or no exercise.

AMAZING BUT TRUE!

A massive feat of endurance

In 2007, horse rider Claire Lomas had a terrible fall that badly damaged her spine. Her legs were totally paralyzed (unable to move) from the waist down. However, she still gets plenty of exercise. She has already learned to ski down black (very difficult) runs using a specially designed chair. Now she is learning to walk wearing a robotic suit, which allows her to use the muscles of her upper body to control the movement of her legs. After a few weeks of training, she managed to walk the length of a room. She is now planning to use the suit to walk the 26 miles (42 kilometers) of the London Marathon.

Storing up problems

Although top athletes reach their peak potential in young adulthood, most young adults do far less exercise than when they were younger. This is the time when most people move away from home, go to college, get a job, find a partner, and have children. All these new experiences and responsibilities can leave little time for exercise.

Young, healthy adults do not usually worry about their health in the future. But the things that young people do at this time of life can affect their health when they are older.

When they first live by themselves, young adults often eat less well than they did living at home. They may also drink more alcohol, and some young adults may smoke. Smoking, drinking too much, and eating a poor diet may not have immediate effects. But they can lead to obesity, increases in blood pressure, and higher levels of cholesterol in the blood. In middle age, people who are overweight have high blood pressure or high cholesterol levels and are at greater risk of having a heart attack, a stroke, or suffering from kidney damage (see pages 46 and 47).

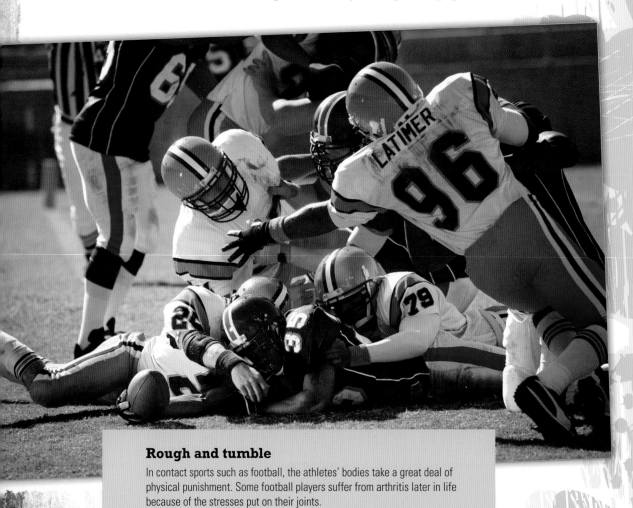

Rough and tumble
In contact sports such as football, the athletes' bodies take a great deal of physical punishment. Some football players suffer from arthritis later in life because of the stresses put on their joints.

Measuring intensity

No matter what the activity is, if your heart rate increases, you start to sweat, and you work your muscles more than they are used to, then you are getting benefits from the exercise. A rough way to measure exercise intensity is by seeing how breathless you are. If you can talk but not sing, the exercise is moderately intensive. If you can only say a few words before pausing to breathe, then the exercise is vigorous.

Different kinds of exercise

One way for young adults to find space for regular exercise is to find different kinds of exercise that fit in better with their lives. For example, dog owners could take their dog for a run or even a bike ride, rather than letting it off the leash and throwing a ball. Parents with babies over six months old can get good exercise by taking the baby with them on a run using a jogging stroller. Going to run errands on a bike rather than in a car can be good exercise, as can digging in a garden.

Finding new ways to exercise

Young children make heavy demands on their parents, and the parents may find it difficult to exercise the way they used to. They may have to find new ways to keep themselves fit.

Checking fitness

If you are exercising regularly, you can check your progress using your pulse rate. Find out your resting pulse rate by measuring it several times. Take your pulse right after exercise, then take your "recovery pulse" two minutes later. As you get fitter, you should recover from exercise more quickly, so your recovery pulse rate will go down.

Middle Adulthood to Old Age: Slowing Down, but Not Much!

As we get older, we begin to lose the peak speed, power, and agility we had as young adults. From about age 30, the body begins to slow down gradually.

The following are some of the changes that begin to happen in the middle adult years.

Wrinkles and muscles

Some of the most obvious signs of getting older are the wrinkles that begin to appear on the face. These are caused by the fact that the skin begins to lose its elasticity as we get older. Another obvious sign of getting older is that, for some people, the hair starts to thin and it may turn gray.

Wrinkles and hair thinning do not affect people's physical performance, but other changes do. From about the age of 30, people begin to lose muscle mass. This is because older people are not as good at making muscle protein from food, and also because the system that stops muscles from being broken down is not as good as it is in younger people.

Muscle loss is slow at first. If exercise levels stay at around the same level, there is little effect between the ages of about 30 and 40. However, by the age of 50, people begin to lose muscle mass, and by 65 they have only about three-quarters of the muscle that they had in their twenties.

In addition to losing power, people lose some range of movement as they get older. Muscles and tendons become less stretchy and joints stiffen up.

Do we really get weaker?

One problem with studying how people change as they get older is that most people exercise less in middle age than they did when they were younger. Are the changes that scientists measure real, or do people have less muscle because they got less fit as they got older?

One study addressed this problem by looking at weight lifting and power lifting records for people of different ages. They found that the record weight lifted gradually dropped as people got older, compared to the record for the open class (any age). The results were similar for both males and females.

Record-breaking weight lifters and power lifters must train hard in order to make record-breaking lifts. So, this study showed that even if older people train hard, they do not have the same strength and power as top lifters who are younger.

Endurance versus sprint performance

There are differences in how fast performance drops off in sprint events compared to endurance events. Sprint times for men start to drop off by the time they are in their forties. Women seem to slow down a little later. By the age of 60, both men and women are nearly two seconds slower over 100 meters than when they were younger. Above the age of 60, people's speed starts to drop more quickly.

Performance in endurance events does not drop off as fast as it does for sprints. People are still able to run good marathon times, for example, in their seventies.

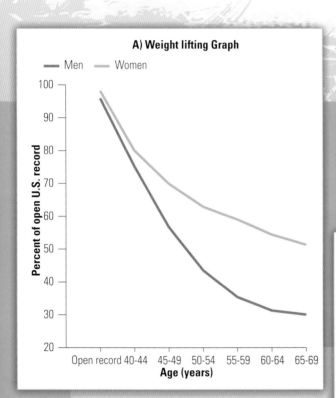

A) Weight lifting Graph

— Men   — Women

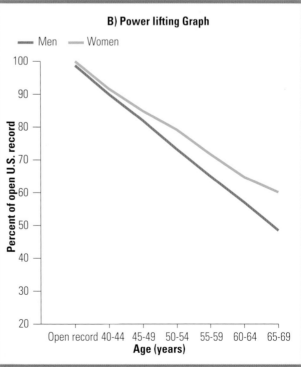

B) Power lifting Graph

— Men   — Women

Less strength

These graphs show how the weight lifting (top) and power lifting (right) record lifts are reduced as men and women get older.

Heart and weight

The heart does not perform as well in middle age as it does when people are younger. Cardiac output (the amount of blood that the heart can pump in a minute) and maximum heart rate are both reduced with age. The overall effects of changes in the heart and circulation mean that people's maximum aerobic power (the maximum amount of power produced in aerobic exercise) falls by about 1 percent per year, on average.

As people lose muscle, bodies also gain weight. Weight gain starts from about the age of 18, but in the twenties the changes are small and are mainly due to an increase in muscle. As people get older, weight continues to increase, even though people have less muscle. Most of the extra weight is due to an increase in fat.

The nerves and senses

Aging affects the nervous system as much as other parts of the body. The speed at which people react slows down, and the fingers and hands lose agility. These changes affect many activities, because we need fast reactions to catch a ball or dodge past a defender, for example.

The senses are less acute in middle age. Many people have difficulty reading small print in books and magazines, because their eyes have "stiffened up" and they can no longer focus as well. As people get older, they also lose the ability to hear very high-pitched sounds.

Exercise for all
Walking, gardening, or dancing are all effective forms of exercise in middle age.

Exercise helps

The changes that develop in people's bodies as they get older happen to everyone. They are part of a more general loss of efficiency in the way the body takes care of itself. For example, the body is less good at keeping a constant temperature and at maintaining the correct levels of important chemicals such as glucose in the blood. However, the rate at which these changes happen can be very different among individuals. One person might begin to lose his hair or go gray in his twenties, while another may have a full head of hair in his sixties.

Some of the differences in how people age are genetic. They are a result of the mix of genes that people inherited from their parents. However, lifestyle can have a big effect on the speed at which aging changes happen. Many studies have shown that for people who get regular exercise, changes due to aging happen more slowly. If middle-aged people get plenty of exercise, they will lose muscle more slowly, and the changes in the heart will happen more slowly.

Older gold

Some athletes can continue to perform at their peak for many years. Rower Steve Redgrave won his fifth Olympic gold medal in 2000, at the age of 38.

AMAZING BUT TRUE!

Death-defying exercise

Exercise in middle age can save you from death! A study at the University of Michigan looked at benefits of exercise for middle-aged people. In a group of 9,611 adults, researchers found that those who were regularly active in their fifties and early sixties were about 35 percent less likely to die within eight years than those who got no exercise. It is this sort of evidence that shows that exercising really does make a big difference.

Core stability

As we saw earlier (see page 13), in the first year of life we develop the muscles we need to stand upright and walk. The muscles develop from the center of the body outward. The first of these muscles to develop are those in the torso. These are our core muscles.

If people stay active throughout their lives, the core muscles stay strong and do their job of keeping the body stable and linking together the upper and lower body. They can help give good posture. However, years of sitting at desks and in front of computer screens mean that many people have weak core muscles that cannot do their job properly. This affects any kind of exercise. If the core muscles are not doing their job, other muscles have to work harder and may become overstrained. This causes problems such as back strain, which affect many people. Weak core muscles can lead to poor physical performance.

In the past 30 or 40 years, sports scientists have begun to understand the importance of the core muscles and how core stability can improve physical ability and help to avoid injuries. Sports coaches have developed many exercises to improve core stability. These often involve doing exercises sitting or lying on a large exercise ball or standing on a wobble cushion (also called a stability disc). The idea is that the ball or cushion makes a person slightly unstable. The body has to make small corrections to keep balanced, and this is very good for core stability.

Test your core stability

Try this test to see how good your core stability is. If your core muscles are not strong, they will quickly tire and you will not be able to do the whole exercise.

You will need:

- a nonslip mat
- a watch or clock with a second hand

You could get someone to help with the timing. Perhaps you could have a core stability challenge with some of your friends.

1. Start in the plank position (see the artwork at right). Hold this for 30 seconds.

2. Lift your right arm off the ground and hold for 10 seconds.

3. Put your right arm down and lift the left. Hold for 10 seconds.

4. Put your left arm down and lift your right leg off the ground. Hold for 10 seconds.

5. Put your right leg down and repeat with your left leg.

6. Lift your left leg and right arm off the ground. Hold for 10 seconds.

7. Repeat with your right leg and left arm.

8. Return to the plank position and hold for 15 seconds.

Once you can do this comfortably, increase the time you hold each position.

Many top athletes now include core stability exercises as part of their training, because strong core muscles give the limbs a stable center to work from.

1. **Plank position**
   Support your weight on your forearms and toes as shown. Your body should form a straight line from your shoulders to your ankles. Your lower abdomen and back work to keep your body straight. Hold for one minute.

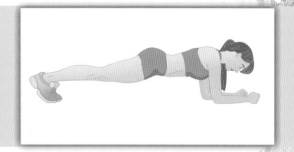

2. **Leg and back lift**
   Lie on your back with your knees bent and your feet flat on the floor. Lift your pelvis so that your body forms a straight line from your shoulders to knees. Lift your right leg off the floor and extend it so that it continues the straight line. Hold for 30 seconds, then repeat with your left leg.

3. **"Superman"**
   Balance on the floor on your hands and knees. Your back should be flat and parallel to the floor. Now stretch your right arm out in front and your left leg out behind, keeping them straight. Hold for 30 seconds, then repeat on the other side.

4. **Fitness ball "crunch"**
   Sit on the ball and then walk your feet away while going down into a lying position. The ball should be under your lower back. Your feet should be flat on the floor and your knees at a 90-degree angle. Place your hands across your chest (beginner) or behind your head (intermediate or advanced). You should now be in the position shown in the diagram top right. To start a crunch, slightly curl your head, neck, and shoulders toward your pelvis. Pause for a second at the top of the move (see diagram bottom right), then slowly return to the start. Repeat as many times as you can. This is a crunch, not a sit-up, so you should move only a couple of inches each time.

Old age

As people move from middle age into their sixties and seventies, physical performance begins to drop off more quickly. Older people start to lose more muscle fibers, so that by the age of 80 people may have lost 40 to 50 percent of their total muscle mass. At a certain point, this loss of strength can start to affect everyday life. Older people who have lost a lot of muscle may no longer be able to open a jar or get up from a chair without help, for example.

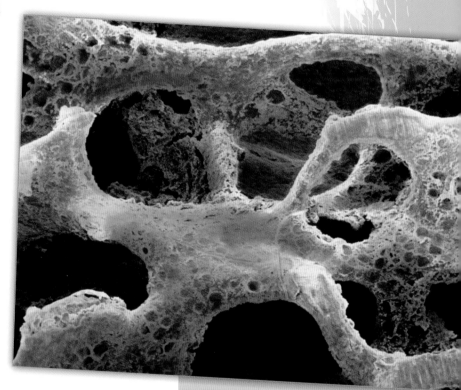

Bones lose strength and mass in a similar way to the muscles. The bones gradually begin to lose calcium and other **minerals**. These are the ingredients that give bones their hardness and much of their strength. As they lose minerals, the bones gradually become spongy and weak. This is known as osteoporosis. In people with serious osteoporosis, a very mild fall or even a bout of coughing can cause a bone to fracture (break), and at this age bone fractures can take a very long time to heal. Older people may also have problems with arthritis when it becomes painful or difficult to move the joints.

Spongy bones

This micrograph shown a close-up of bones with osteoporosis. The bone tissue is low in calcium (which gives the bones strength) and full of air spaces.

More illness

As people get older, the heart and lungs, the nervous system, the senses, and other organs decline in a similar way to the muscles and bones. People may suffer from heart problems, vascular disease ("furring up" of the blood vessels), asthma, liver and kidney problems, and all kinds of infections. Older people also take longer to recover from illness or injury.

Continuing exercise

Exercise can be hard for older people, and if they have joint problems, it may be painful. But recent research has shown that in nearly all cases, exercise brings benefits:

- For people at risk of heart disease, exercise helps increase aerobic capacity.

- Exercise can help reduce levels of fats in the blood, which reduces the risk of vascular disease.

- Gentle exercise, preferably in a warm swimming pool, can improve joint movement in people with arthritis.

Regular load-bearing or resistance exercise can slow down or halt the loss of minerals from the bones and even to some extent reverse mineral loss. This is a particular problem for females after **menopause**.

Resistance training brings improvements in strength.

Researchers have found that just eight weeks of resistance training exercises can produce significant improvements in strength and health for people in their eighties. Exercises could include squats (sitting and standing using a chair), press-ups against a wall, and bicep curls using small weights.

Keeping up the resistance

Resistance exercises such as rowing continue to be good for people well into old age.

AMAZING BUT TRUE!

Sixty-five and still improving

Since 2002, U.S. cyclist Bob Unger has trained hard to improve his cycling performance. Every so often, he has a series of tests conducted to check his heart rate, VO$_2$ max, and other measures of fitness. In a fitness test in August 2011, at the age of 65, his VO$_2$ max and his exercise recovery were better than they were in his first tests nine years earlier. His improvement shows that it is possible to get fitter at an age when the body is supposed to be in decline.

An added bonus

Exercise for older people does not just have physical benefits. There is good evidence that older people who exercise enjoy life more. Exercise helps people to get out and meet others and to do something they enjoy. It makes people feel good and gives them a sense of achievement.

Overall, there has been a major change in attitudes toward exercise for older people, both among experts and among older people themselves. In the past, people thought that exercise in old age was risky and could shorten a person's life. Today, there is plenty of evidence that the opposite is true. Exercise helps people to live longer and prevents them from getting sick. People at high risk of conditions such as heart disease, and even people recovering from serious illness, also get benefits from a program of regular exercise combined with adequate rest.

Governments in most of the more economically developed countries have recommendations for how much exercise older people should be doing. The recommended healthy level of exercise for those over the age of 65 is at least 2 1/2 hours of moderate exercise per week, or 1 1/4 hours of vigorous exercise per week. Each exercise session should be no less than 10 minutes long. This should include at least two activities that build muscle strength, for example exercising with weights. It should also include some aerobic exercise, to get the heart pumping and increase the breathing rate. Activities such as fast walking, biking, and swimming are good aerobic exercises for older people.

Activities that improve balance and coordination, such as yoga or Tai Chi, can greatly reduce the risk of slipping and falling. This is important for older people as they are more likely to be badly hurt or break a bone in a fall.

Getting active

The benefits of exercise for older people are really clear. However, if people have spent years without getting much exercise, it can be hard to get going.

One place for older people to start is with an activity diary. What activities do they do each day? How much exercise does this add up to in a week? Some guidelines suggest that older people should do at least two and a half hours of moderate exercise per week. There should be a mix of aerobic (endurance) exercise and exercise to build strength.

Once older people know how much exercise they get already, they can look at ways of increasing it and set some goals. Maybe they could spend 30 minutes doing some gardening each week or join a group that does ballroom dancing. Perhaps they could agree to go for a brisk 10-minute walk each day with a friend. Older people should choose things they will enjoy doing, not activities that feel like a chore.

If older people are already active, there is always room for improvement, like adding progression (see page 39) to their exercise routine.

Morning workout

In the parks in Beijing, China, thousands of older people start the day practicing Tai Chi. The slow, controlled movements of Tai Chi look easy, but done properly Tai Chi is very good exercise for the legs and keeps the heart and blood system healthy.

AMAZING BUT TRUE!

Doesn't seem a day older

As bodies get older, they "wear out." So, it seems like common sense that older people are more likely to die than those who are younger.

However, in the 1990s, scientists unearthed a surprising discovery— something that was first observed in the 1930s. They found that for people who survive beyond 90 years old, mortality (death) rates seem to stop rising. This does not mean that people over 90 do not die. But it does mean that they stop getting older, physically. So, a 90-year-old has as much chance of making it to 100 as an 80-year-old has of reaching 90.

Full of potential

Older people usually prefer to try gentler kinds of exercise than they did when they were younger. But not American Lew Hollander. In 2010, he was 80 years old, but he showed no signs of slowing down. He was the oldest competitor in the World Ironman Championship that year. This involved swimming 2.4 miles (3.8 kilometers), biking 112 miles (180 kilometers), then running a marathon (26.2 miles, or 42.2 kilometers). He did the whole thing in 15 hours, 48 minutes, and 40 seconds.

Hollander is obviously an exceptional athlete. Most 20-year-olds could not have matched his performance. But he is not alone. The world-record marathon time for the over-seventies is 2 hours, 54 minutes, and 49 seconds, set by 73-year-old Ed Whitlock from Canada. His time puts him in the top 2 percent of marathon runners in the world, regardless of age.

Runner for life

This older athlete is running in the Boston Marathon in 2008.

People like Whitlock and Hollander show that older people can maintain an impressive amount of cardiovascular fitness into their seventies and eighties. As with people in middle age, older people perform much better in endurance events than in sprint-style, anaerobic activities. However, this does not mean that they should focus only on aerobic training. Hollander includes a lot of anaerobic training in his exercise routines.

Other older athletes

The following are more examples of outstanding older athletes:

- *Merlene Ottey*: This sprinter, originally from Jamaica, ran in the 4-x-400-meter relay team for Slovenia in the 2010 European Championships, at the age of 50.

- *Dorothy de Low*: This Australian table tennis player competed in the World Veterans Table Tennis Championships of 2001, at the age of 100.

- *Hiroshi Hoketsu*: This horse rider was a member of the Japanese Olympic team in Beijing, China, in 2008, at age 67.

- *Frankie Manning*: She toured the world teaching and demonstrating the Lindy Hop (a type of dance), at the age of 92.

- *Lucille Borgen*: She competed in the U.S. National Waterskiing Championships, at the age of 94.

- *Barbara Hillary*: In 2007, this American became the oldest person to reach the North Pole, at the age of 75.

Exercise from birth to death

The old view of physical development was that we grow and develop quickly until we become young adults. After this peak in physical ability, the decline begins and we can gradually do less and less. However, newer studies, and the growing numbers of very fit, active older people, have shown that this story is too simple. If we stay active and keep exercising, we can slow down the decline and even perhaps reverse it. Moreover, improvements in medicine and public health mean that young people today can expect to live longer than their parents. Who knows? Perhaps it won't be long before 100-year-olds are regularly running marathons and competing in Ironman events. Maybe you will be one of them!

Quiz

Find out how much you remember about the benefits of exercise throughout our lives by completing this quiz. You will find the answers on page 63.

1. What is the most important nutrient for your muscles?
  a.) protein   b.) glucose   c.) fructose   d.) sucrose

2. This diagram shows a muscle, bone, and joint working together as a lever. What does this lever do?
  a.) magnify the force of the muscle
  b.) turn a short movement of the muscle into a bigger movement of the bone

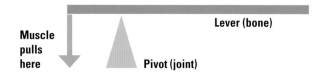

3. When you start to exercise, what happens to your heart and circulatory system?
  a.) your heart beats slower and more strongly, and your blood vessels contract
  b.) your heart beats faster, and more blood flows to your digestive system
  c.) your heart beats faster and more strongly, and blood flow increases
  d.) your heart slows, and blood flow is reduced

4.. What happens to your respiratory system during exercise?
  a.) you breathe fast and more shallowly, so more carbon dioxide gets into your blood
  b.) you breathe faster and more deeply, so that more oxygen gets into the lungs
  c.) you breathe more slowly but deeply, so that your lungs can take in less oxygen
  d.) you breathe faster, and blood flows into the spaces in the lungs

5. Can you put these milestones in the order they usually happen?
  They are: rolling, tying shoelaces, crawling, reaching, talking, walking.

6. Which of these animals has helped to improve swimsuit design?
  a.) shark   b.) tuna   c.) hippo   d.) meerkat

7. Which of these things does a warm-up NOT do?
  a.) helps prevent muscle stiffness and injury
  b.) gets blood flow going
  c.) warms muscle
  d.) improves strength

8. In South Asia and Africa especially, many children under five do not get the basic things they need for the healthy development of their bodies and brains. Name two of the things that they need.

9. There are several different types of fitness. Can you name four of them?

10. What is your favorite sport or type of exercise? What are the most important types of fitness for this sport? Research or think of an exercise for each of these types of fitness.

11. How old was Nadia Comaneci when she won Olympic gold in 1976?
a.) 13   b.) 14   c.) 15   d.) 16

12. How old was Merlene Ottey when she ran in the 4-x-400-meter relay in the 2010 European Championships?
a.) 3   b.) 40   c.) 50   d.) 60

13. What is the name for the changes in the body that begin to happen at around age 10 for girls, and a little later for boys?
a.) puberty   b.) menopause   c.) obsolescence   d.) adulation

14. Did the changes connected to puberty begin earlier or later in the 19th century?

15. Can you think of three benefits of regular exercise?

16. What type of muscles are most useful for a sprinter to have? How can people get more of this type of muscle?

17. Overload, progression, individuality, specificity, recovery—what do these words describe?
a.) the main stages of child development
b.) the main phases of a circuit training session
c.) four types of running shorts
d.) the basic principles of fitness training

18. What is the plank position good for?
a.) woodworking   b.) improving core stability
c.) making a person very stiff   d.) improving flexibility

Timeline of Physical Development

Age	Milestone
1 month	Head droops without support Grasps objects placed in hands Sucks objects placed in mouth Sleeps about 16 hours a day
4 months	Doubles birth weight Almost no head droop while in a sitting position Able to sit straight if propped up Able to roll from front to back Can hold and let go of an object Sleeps 9 to 10 hours at night with two naps (total of 14 to 16 hours per day)
9 months	Gains weight at a slower rate—about 0.5 ounces (15 grams) per day Is able to crawl Sits for long periods Pulls self to standing position Throws or shakes objects Responds to name Plays interactive games, such as peek-a-boo and patty cake
12 months	Triples birth weight Has one to eight teeth Pulls to stand Walks with help or alone Sits down without help Sleeps 8 to 10 hours a night and takes one to two naps Responds to his or her name Understands several words Can say "mamma," "dada," and at least one or two other words Points to objects with index finger
18 months	Is growing at a slower rate and has less of an appetite compared to months before Is able to control the muscles used to urinate and have bowel movements (sphincter muscles), but may not be ready to use the toilet Runs with a lack of coordination and falls often Is able to get onto small chairs without help Walks up stairs while holding on with one hand Can build a tower of two to four blocks Can say 10 or more words when asked Is able to take off some clothing items, such as gloves, hats, and socks

Age	Milestone
2 years	Can turn a doorknob Can kick a ball without losing balance Can pick up objects while standing, without losing balance Can run with better coordination May be ready for toilet training Able to put on simple clothes without help Vocabulary of 50 to 300 words Can organize phrases of two to three words Vision is fully developed
2 years	Has improved balance Has improved vision (20/30) Has all 20 primary teeth (baby teeth) Needs 11 to 13 hours of sleep a day Can briefly balance on one foot May walk up the stairs with alternating feet (without holding the railing) Can pedal a tricycle Can dress self, only requiring assistance with laces, buttons, and other fasteners Has some cooperative play (building tower of blocks together)
3 years	Grows to a height that is double the length at birth Shows improved balance Hops on one foot without losing balance Throws a ball overhand with coordination Can cut out a picture using scissors May not be able to tie shoelaces Has a vocabulary of more than 1,000 words
5 years	Gains about 4.5 pounds (2 kilograms) per year Grows about 5 to 7 inches (13 to 18 centimeters) per year Vision has reached 20/20 The first permanent teeth may erupt (most children do not get their first permanent teeth until age 6) Developing increased coordination Skipping, jumping, and hopping with good balance Maintaining balance while standing on one foot with eyes closed Can count to 10

Age	Milestone
6 to 10 years	Smooth and strong motor skills Coordination (especially hand–eye), endurance, balance, and physical abilities vary More social—more likely to enjoy team activities Able to understand and act on physical instructions—can benefit from coaching/training
Puberty	In girls, ovaries begin to increase production of estrogen and other female hormones. In boys, testicles increase production of testosterone. These and other hormones produce the physical changes found in puberty.
Girls:	Development of breasts Increase in height Increase in hip size Pubic, armpit, and leg hair growth Menstrual cycles occur over about 1 month (28 to 32 days)
Boys:	Faster growth, especially height Hair growth under the arms, on the face, and in the pubic area Increased shoulder width Growth of the penis, scrotum (with reddening and folding of the skin), and testes Voice deepens
Young adulthood (18–30)	Peak physical development Strength increases into late twenties Some loss of hearing high pitches by late twenties
Older adulthood (31+)	Hair may gray and thin Eyes less able to focus over full range; may need glasses (presbyopia) Women undergo menopause (egg production ceases) Manual dexterity begins to reduce in mid-thirties Progressive loss of muscle strength Slower loss of endurance performance Bones lose minerals and are less strong, with lower mass Weight generally increases and there is a greater proportion of fat tissue Reaction times slow More risk of heart and lung problems

Exercise for different types of fitness

Aerobic exercises

Moderate effort
(working hard enough to raise your heart rate and break a sweat)

- walking to school
- playing in the playground
- skateboarding
- rollerblading
- walking the dog
- riding a bike on level ground or with few hills
- pushing a lawn mower

Vigorous-intensity
(breathing hard and fast, heart rate high)

- playing tag
- energetic dancing
- aerobics
- running
- gymnastics
- playing soccer
- martial arts such as karate
- riding a bike fast or on hills

Muscle-strengthening activities

- games such as tug-of-war
- rope climbing
- sit-ups
- push-ups
- swinging on playground equipment or bars
- gymnastics
- resistance exercises with exercise bands, weight machines, or hand-held weights
- rock climbing

Bone-strengthening activities

- games such as hopscotch
- hopping, skipping, and jumping
- jumping rope
- running
- sports such as gymnastics, soccer, volleyball, and tennis

Glossary

adolescence period in development when young people become adults. Puberty refers to the physical changes that happen during adolescence.

adolescent young person in adolescence, between the ages of about 13 and 19

aerobic respiration series of chemical reactions inside cells that produce energy from the sugar glucose. Aerobic respiration needs oxygen to work.

anaerobic respiration series of chemical reactions to get energy from glucose that do not need oxygen. This type of respiration produces far less energy than aerobic respiration.

arthritis inflammation (swelling), stiffness, and pain in the joints

carbon dioxide gas found in the air that is also a waste product of respiration

cell very small, membrane-bound structures that are the basic building blocks of living things

center of gravity single point on an object where all its mass could be concentrated without affecting its behavior. An object can be balanced on its center of gravity.

cholesterol fatty substance found in the bloodstream. Cholesterol is important for building new cells, but too much cholesterol in the blood can increase the risk of heart problems.

circulatory system organ system made up of the heart, blood, and blood vessels

contract shorten

coordination way in which muscles work together to produce a desired movement

core muscles deep muscles of the stomach and back, responsible for maintaining posture

diabetes disorder in which the body cannot properly control the levels of sugar in the blood. High blood sugar levels cause damage to the eyes, the kidneys and the nervous system.

digestive system organ system made up of the stomach, intestines, and other organs involved in the digestion of food

drag force on an object moving through a fluid (a liquid or a gas) that tends to slow down the object

gene section of DNA (genetic material) that carries the information to make a particular protein

genetic relating to genes

gland group of special cells in the body that produces particular chemicals and releases them

glucose simple sugar that is the main source of energy in the cells of humans and other animals

hormone substance that is produced in one part of the body, then travels in the bloodstream to one or more target areas, where it has an effect

joint connection between two or more bones. Joints such as the shoulder or the hip have a wide range of movement. Others, such as the joints in the skull, hardly move at all.

lever rigid bar pivoted at one point. A force on one side of the pivot (the load) produces a movement and a force (the effort) on the other side.

ligament tough, fibrous tissue that connects bones

menopause time in a woman's life when she stops producing eggs

mineral simple, inorganic chemical found in soil and in most kinds of foods

nervous system organ system made up of the brain, spinal cord, and nerves. Together, they make a system for sending messages rapidly around the body.

nutrient simple substance that can be used by the body to provide energy, or for growth and repair

obese very overweight

obesity being very overweight

organ part of the body in which a group of tissues work together to carry out a particular job. For example, the heart is the organ that pumps blood around the body.

organ system group of organs that work together to fulfill a particular function in the body—for example, breathing or carrying blood around the body

posture way in which a person stands and moves

puberty time in people's development when they become able to reproduce (have babies)

reflex fast reaction to a stimulus that involves the spinal cord but not the brain

reproductive organ organ in the body that is involved in sexual reproduction

resistance training fitness training in which weights or other devices are used to resist the contraction of muscles and so make them work harder

respiratory system organ system that includes the mouth, throat, lungs, and other organs involved in breathing and gas exchange (getting oxygen into the blood and carbon dioxide out)

skeletal system structure of bones and cartilage that functions to support the body

spinal cord thick bundle of nerve tissue that runs down the middle of the spinal column

stimulus (plural: stimuli) something that produces a reaction. For example, bright light is a stimulus to the pupil of the eye, which reacts by becoming smaller.

strength training exercise that aims to strengthen the muscles

stroke condition in which for some reason the blood supply to part of the brain is interrupted (stopped for a time). This causes the death of some brain cells in the area, which can cause all kinds of brain disorders.

tendon strong, slightly elastic cord that connects muscles to bones

tissue grouping of similar cells that performs a function. Muscle tissue, for example, is made up of bundles of muscle cells (muscle fibers).

$VO_{2\ max}$ amount of oxygen that a person uses when they are exercising at their absolute maximum. The $VO_{2\ max}$ is one of the best measures of aerobic fitness.

Find Out More

Books

Ballard, Carol. *Keeping Fit: Body Systems* (*Do It Yourself*).
   Chicago: Heinemann Library, 2008.

Hardyman, Robyn. *Exercise* (*Being Healthy, Feeling Great*).
   New York: PowerKids, 2010.

Sheen, Barbara. *Girls' Guide to Feeling Fabulous!* (*Life Skills*).
   Chicago: Heinemann Library, 2009.

Spilsbury, Louise. *Why Should I Get Off the Couch? And Other Questions About Health and
   Exercise* (*InfoSearch*). Chicago: Heinemann Library, 2003.

Townsend, John. *101 Things You Didn't Know About Your Body* (*101*).
   Chicago: Raintree, 2012.

Web sites

www.cdc.gov/ncbddd/childdevelopment/
Learn more about child development from the U.S. Centers for Disease Control and
Prevention (CDC).

www.cdc.gov/physicalactivity/everyone/guidelines/children.html
The CDC offers some guidelines on getting active, including the diaries of two typical
active children.

kidshealth.org/kid/stay_healthy/index.html
Kidshealth offers a clear, fun guide to staying healthy, with illustrations and animations.

www.letsmove.gov
Let's Move! is a U.S. government program aimed at encouraging young people to get active.
First Lady Michelle Obama launched this program.

pbskids.org/itsmylife/body/index.html
This PBS site has information on a range of subjects, including food choices and puberty.

Places to visit

The Exploratorium
3601 Lyon Street
San Francisco, California 94123
www.exploratorium.edu
The museum allows kids to learn all
about the human body.

The Health Museum
1515 Hermann Drive
Houston, Texas 77004
www.mhms.org
This museum offers interactive exhibits
about the body and health.

Topics to research

A balanced diet

Diet and exercise are closely linked. You need energy to exercise, and this energy comes from food. So find out more about food. What needs to be in a balanced diet?

Find out what some top athletes eat. Is their diet different from the diet of an ordinary person? If so, why is it different?

Fitness testing

We saw on page 23 that there are several different kinds of fitness. Find out about fitness testing. Can you find a test for each kind of fitness?

Try out your fitness tests. How fit are you? How fit are your friends, or people in your class? You might find that some people do well on one kind of test and not so well on another. So what does fitness really mean?

Quiz answers (see pages 56–57)

1) b.

2) b.

3) c.

4) b.

5) Reaching, rolling, crawling, walking, talking, tying shoelaces.

6) a.

7) d.

8) Correct answers include: Enough food, specific nutrients (such as iron), exercise, and education.

9) Correct answers include: Endurance, strength, power, speed, agility, flexibility, coordination, and balance.

10) This is an open question.

11) b.

12) c.

13) a.

14) They occurred later in the 19th century.

15) Correct answers include: That it keeps your weight down, boosts energy, combats illness, helps you sleep, less risk of early death, and cheers you up.

16) Fast-twitch muscles are most useful. A person cannot get more of this muscle; the relative proportions of fast-twitch and slow-twitch muscles are genetically determined.

17) d.

18) b.

Index

adolescence 26, 27, 28, 29, 32, 34

aerobic respiration 10, 40, 46, 51, 52, 55, 59

agility 23, 24, 25, 38, 39, 44, 46

anaerobic respiration 30–31, 55

arteries 9, 37

arthritis 25, 37, 42, 50, 51

balance 14, 15, 18, 20, 23, 24, 48, 52, 58, 59

benefits 5, 16, 24, 29, 36–37, 43, 47, 51, 52

birth 12, 27

BMI ("body mass index") 34, 35

bones See skeletal system.

carbon dioxide 9, 10, 11

cardiac output 46

cells 7, 8, 9, 10, 11, 27, 31

center of gravity 18, 24

cerebellum 6

cheerleading 24

circuit training 21

circulatory system 5, 7, 8, 9, 10, 11, 16, 33, 36, 37, 40, 43, 46, 47, 50, 51, 53

coordination 15, 16, 18, 20, 23, 38, 52, 58, 59

core muscles 13, 48–49

cycling 10, 11, 19, 40, 51, 52, 54

deaths 33, 37, 47, 53

developed countries 4, 5, 52

digestive system 7, 8, 9

diseases. See illnesses.

drag 17

education 18

endorphins 37

endurance 23, 40–41, 45, 55, 59

energy 5, 6–7, 8, 10, 11, 31, 33, 36, 37, 40

epithelium 8

fast-twitch muscles 31, 41

flexibility 16, 23, 24, 25, 29, 39

food 4, 6–7, 8, 9, 10, 18, 33, 34, 44

genetics 31, 47

glucose 7, 10, 11, 31, 33, 47

glycogen 11

government campaigns 35

gymnastics 21, 23, 24, 25, 39, 59

heart. See circulatory system.

heptathlons 39

hormones 27, 28

illnesses 5, 25, 33, 34, 36, 37, 38, 50, 51, 52

joints 6, 7, 8, 16, 18, 22, 23, 25, 34, 37, 44, 50, 51

lactic acid 31

leg muscles 11, 13, 15

levers 7

ligaments 8, 13, 25

lungs. See respiratory system.

maximal oxygen uptake. See VO2 max.

mechanical advantage 7

molecules 7

mood swings 28

movement advantage 7

muscular system 6, 7, 8, 10, 13, 15, 16, 31, 39, 40, 41, 44, 48, 50, 58, 59

nervous system 6, 9, 46, 50

nutrients 7, 9, 18

obesity 5, 29, 33, 34–35, 36, 42

Olympic Games 17, 24, 30, 47, 55

osteoporosis 50

oxygen 7, 9, 10, 11, 30, 31, 40, 41

paralysis 41

playing 18, 19, 20, 22, 36

progression 39, 52

puberty 26, 27, 28, 29, 32, 38, 59

pulse rate 43

reflexes 12, 13, 14

relaxation 32, 33, 34

resistance training 29, 44, 51

respiration 10, 11, 30, 31, 40

respiratory system 7, 9, 10, 11, 16, 40, 43, 50, 59

robots 15, 41

safety 22, 25

secondary sex characteristics 27

senses 20, 46, 50

serotonin 37

skeletal system 6, 7, 8, 24, 28, 29, 31, 34, 50, 51, 59

skiing 40, 41, 55

skills 19, 20, 21, 24, 38

skin-fold tests 34, 35

slow-twitch muscles 31, 41

speed 23, 30, 40, 41, 44, 45, 46, 47

sports 17, 20, 21, 22, 23, 24, 25, 30, 31, 38, 39, 40, 41, 47, 48, 54, 55, 59

sprinting 23, 30, 31, 40, 41, 45, 55

strength 18, 23, 24, 25, 38, 44, 45, 50, 59

strength training 5, 21, 51, 52, 59

stretching 24, 25

subsistence farmers 4

substance abuse 28, 42

swimming 12, 16–17, 21, 23, 39, 52, 54

Tai Chi 52, 53

teenagers. See adolescence.

tendons 8, 25, 44

tissues 8, 31, 34

toddlers 18, 19, 22, 58

Tour de France 40

VO$_2$ max (maximal oxygen uptake) 41, 51

walking 13, 14, 15, 16, 18, 36, 48, 49, 52

warm-up exercises 17

water 10, 16, 17, 34

weight training. See resistance training.

wheelchair basketball 21

World Health Organization 33

World Ironman Championship 54